FORGIVENESS, SET YOUR SPIRIT FREE!!!

Forgiveness, Set your Spirit Free!!!

Susette ONeal

Contents

Title Page

Forgiveness: *Set your Spirit Free*

BY SUSETTE A. O'NEAL

Copyright Page

Dedication

DEDICATION

Inspired by the remarkable tales of forgiveness woven by historical icons such as Nelson Mandela, Mahatma Gandhi, and spiritual luminaries like the Dalai Lama, I dedicate this book. As a woman of profound faith, guided by the teachings of Jesus Christ, I understand the profound impact of prayer and forgiveness. My earnest wish is for you to find the courage to extend forgiveness, both to yourself and to others, recognizing that we all may unwittingly inflict harm.

Table of Contents

Acknowledgements

ACKNOWLEDGMENT

I am deeply grateful to my loving family, especially my husband of 37 years and my two wonderful children, for their unwavering support and understanding throughout the process of bringing this book to life. Your encouragement and patience have been my rock. To my friends and colleagues who provided invaluable feedback, encouragement, and inspiration along the way, thank you for believing in me and cheering me on. I would also like to express my gratitude to the readers who have embraced my stories with open hearts. Your enthusiasm and support mean the world to me.

1

Understanding Forgiveness

1 Chapter Understanding Forgiveness

The Definition and Importance of Forgiveness

In our journey through life, forgiveness is an essential and transformative practice that can bring us spiritual freedom and inner peace. It is the act of letting go of resentment, anger, and judgment towards ourselves and others. Forgiveness opens the door to healing, growth, and the restoration of relationships. In this subchapter, we will explore the de1nition and importance of forgiveness in various contexts, from personal development to societal dynamics.

Forgiveness in relationships is the cornerstone of healthy connections. It allows us to release past hurts and rebuild trust, fostering deeper intimacy and understanding. By forgiving, we create space for compassion, empathy, and love to flourish.

Forgiveness in relationships is indeed a fundamental aspect of nurturing healthy connections. It involves letting go of resentment, bitterness, and the desire for revenge after experiencing hurt or betrayal from a partner. Instead of holding onto grudges or dwelling on past grievances, forgiveness enables individuals to move forward with a sense of emotional freedom and openness.

Forgiveness involves acknowledging the pain caused by the actions or words of a partner but choosing to let go of the negative emotions associated with those experiences. It's about freeing oneself from the burden of carrying past grievances and choosing not to let them define the relationship or one's emotional state.

It is essential for rebuilding trust in a relationship. When someone hurts us, it can erode trust, making it difficult to feel secure and vulnerable with that person again. By forgiving, individuals demonstrate a willingness to give their partner another chance and work towards rebuilding a sense of trust and safety in the relationship.

To create an environment conducive to deeper intimacy and connection. forgiveness is essential. When partners are able to forgive each other's mistakes and imperfections, they create space for vulnerability and authenticity in the relationship. This openness allows for greater emotional intimacy and a deeper understanding of each other's needs and desires.

To embrace growth and wholeness, it's essential to let go of lingering hurt and grievances that may have provided a sense of familiarity or a topic for recurring complaints whenever that individual is encountered. Progress demands releasing both the person and the pain they caused, freeing your heart to fully heal and move forward.

It's natural to cling to familiar emotions, even if they're negative, as they provide a sense of identity or validation. However, true healing and personal growth come from breaking free of this cycle, allowing yourself the opportunity to embrace new experiences and relationships without the weight of past grievances.

Forgiveness is not easy and often not comfortable for many. It requires allowing yourself to become vulnerable to that same person that may have hurt you in the past. It involves recognizing the humanity in each other, acknowledging that everyone makes mistakes, and extending grace and understanding even in the face of hurtful actions.

Cultivating these qualities strengthens the emotional bond between partners and promotes mutual respect and kindness.

Ultimately, forgiveness is a catalyst for love to flourish in a relationship. When partners forgive each other and let go of past resentments, they create space for love, acceptance, and growth. Forgiveness allows couples to focus on the present moment and envision a future filled with mutual respect, support, and happiness.

In summary, forgiveness plays a crucial role in fostering healthy and fulfilling relationships by enabling individuals to release past hurts, rebuild trust, deepen intimacy, cultivate compassion and empathy, and allow love to flourish. It's an ongoing process that requires patience, understanding, and a commitment to nurturing the connection between partners.

The Benefits of Forgiveness in Personal and Spiritual Growth

Forgiveness is also a powerful tool for healing trauma. It enables survivors to reclaim their power and move beyond victimhood. By forgiving those who have caused harm, individuals can break free from the chains of pain and find inner peace.

Forgiveness plays a significant role in helping a person discover inner peace by freeing them from the burden of resentment, anger, and negative emotions that can weigh heavily on their psyche.

When a person forgives someone who has wronged them, they release the negative emotions associated with the hurt or betrayal. Holding onto anger, resentment, or bitterness only serves to prolong the pain and keep the individual trapped in a cycle of negativity. Forgiveness allows them to let go of these emotions and experience a sense of relief and emotional freedom.

Forgiveness involves accepting the reality of what has happened and choosing to let go of the desire for things to have been different. By accepting the past and the actions of others, individuals can redirect their focus towards the present moment and future possibilities. This acceptance fosters inner peace by reducing inner conflict and resistance to what cannot be changed.

Holding onto grudges or seeking revenge can consume a significant amount of mental and emotional energy. Forgiveness lightens this burden by releasing the individual from the need to constantly dwell on past grievances or plot retaliation. This mental clarity allows them to redirect their energy towards positive endeavors and personal growth, leading to a greater sense of inner peace.

Forgiveness is not only about pardoning others but also about extending compassion towards oneself. Often, individuals blame themselves for the actions of others or for their own perceived shortcomings. Through forgiveness, they can practice self-compassion by recognizing their humanity, acknowledging their mistakes, and offering themselves the same grace and understanding they extend to others.

Forgiveness shifts the focus from negativity to gratitude and positivity. Instead of dwelling on past hurts, individuals can choose to appreciate the present moment and the blessings in their lives. Cultivating a mindset of gratitude and positivity promotes inner peace by fostering a sense of contentment and fulfillment.

In essence, forgiveness is a powerful tool for cultivating inner peace by releasing negative emotions, promoting acceptance and self-compassion, and fostering emotional healing and positivity. It enables individuals to let go of psychological burdens and embrace a sense of peace and contentment in their lives.

In the realm of self-growth and personal development, forgiveness is a catalyst for transformation. It helps us shed limiting beliefs, resentments, and emotional baggage that hold us back from reaching our full potential. Through forgiveness, we can cultivate self-love, resilience, and a sense of purpose.

Forgiveness also plays a crucial role in healing trauma. When we hold onto past hurts, they can fester within us, causing emotional and physical pain. By forgiving those who have wronged us, we release ourselves from the grip of our traumatic experiences and pave the way for healing and wholeness. Forgiveness enables us to break free from the chains of victimhood and reclaim our personal power.

Susie's Journey

Susie and James had been together for over a decade, building a life filled with love, laughter, and shared dreams. Their bond seemed unbreakable until Susie discovered James's infidelity. The betrayal cut deep, shattering her trust, and leaving her heartbroken.

Despite the pain, Susie was determined to salvage their marriage. She confronted James, demanding answers, and explanations. Tears were shed, words were exchanged, but deep down, Susie still loved him. However, just as they were beginning to rebuild their relationship, another bombshell hit: James had fathered a child with the other woman, Jane.

The revelation was a devastating blow to Susie. She grappled with a whirlwind of emotions - anger, hurt, and profound sadness. How could she ever forgive James for such a profound betrayal?

In the days that followed, Susie found herself at a crossroads. She could either walk away, letting resentment consume her, or she could choose to forgive and fight for what they once had. It wasn't an easy decision. Forgiveness didn't come overnight; it was a process filled with doubts and setbacks.

But as time passed, Susie began to see glimpses of the man she fell in love with - the man who made her laugh, who held her close during tough times, and who shared her hopes and dreams. Despite his flaws and mistakes, she realized that James was still the person she wanted to spend her life with.

With courage and determination, Susie embarked on a journey of forgiveness. She let go of the anger and bitterness that had consumed her, choosing instead to focus on the love they shared and the future they could build together. It wasn't about forgetting or condoning James's actions; it was about choosing to move forward, hand in hand, towards a brighter tomorrow.

Their path was rocky, filled with challenges and doubts, but through it all, Susie and James stood by each other's side. They sought counseling, communicated openly, and worked tirelessly to rebuild trust and strengthen their bond.

Years later, as they celebrated their anniversary, Susie looked at James with gratitude and love. Their journey hadn't been easy, but it had been worth it. In forgiving James, Susie had reclaimed their marriage, forging a love that was stronger and more resilient than ever before.

2

Forgiveness In Relationships

2 Chapter Forgiveness In Relationships

Forgiving Ourselves in Relationships

In our journey through life, we all form relationships with others – be it as parents, children, grandparents, husbands, or wives. These relationships bring us joy, love, and ful1llment, but they can also expose us to pain, hurt, and disappointment. In the midst of these challenges, one of the most crucial aspects of forgiveness is learning to forgive ourselves.

Forgiveness in relationships goes beyond just forgiving others; it involves extending that same compassion and understanding to ourselves. Often, we are quick to blame ourselves for the mistakes we have made or the hurt we have caused. We carry the burden of guilt, shame, and self-condemnation, which can hinder our ability to heal and grow.

In the context of forgiveness, it is essential to recognize that we are all imperfect beings, prone to making mistakes and errors in judgment. It is through these mistakes that we learn, and it is through forgiveness that we find redemption and healing. By forgiving ourselves, we acknowledge our humanity and give ourselves permission to move forward.

Forgiving ourselves in relationships also requires a deep understanding of our own wounds and triggers. It means exploring the root causes of our actions, addressing our own unresolved traumas, and taking responsibility for our own healing. By doing so, we break the cycle of hurt and pain, creating a space for growth and transformation.

For parents and grandparents, forgiving ourselves is crucial in creating a nurturing and loving environment for our children. By modeling self-forgiveness, we teach them the importance of compassion, understanding, and resilience. It allows us to break free from generational patterns of guilt and shame, creating a healthier dynamic for future generations.

In the workplace, forgiving ourselves allows us to embrace our mistakes as opportunities for growth and learning. It fosters an environment of empathy and understanding, where individuals can thrive and reach their full potential. It also enables us to overcome the betrayal we may have experienced and rebuild trust in our relationships.

In the broader societal context, forgiveness plays a vital role in healing cultural and societal wounds. It allows us to acknowledge the pain and injustices of the past, while also moving towards reconciliation and unity. By forgiving ourselves, we contribute to the healing of our communities, fostering a culture of compassion and understanding.

In the journey of self-growth and personal development, forgiveness is a fundamental step towards inner peace and freedom. It liberates us from the shackles of guilt and shame, allowing us to embrace our true selves and live authentically. By forgiving ourselves, we open the door to self-acceptance and self- love.

Ultimately, forgiving ourselves in relationships is an act of self-compassion and self-care. It is a recognition of our worthiness and a commitment to our own well-being. As we extend forgiveness to others, let us not forget the importance of extending it to ourselves as well. By doing so, we unlock the path to spiritual freedom, inner peace, and a more fulfilling life.

Forgiving Others in Relationships

In the realm of relationships, forgiveness plays a pivotal role in cultivating harmony, healing wounds, and fostering growth. Whether we are parents, children, grandparents, husbands, or wives, the act of forgiving others holds immense power to transform our lives and the dynamics within our families.

Forgiveness in relationships is not always easy, but it is a crucial step towards spiritual freedom and inner peace. It requires us to let go of resentment, grudges, and the desire for revenge. Instead, forgiveness allows us to release the emotional baggage that weighs us down and prevents us from experiencing genuine love and connection.

Within the realm of parenting and family dynamics, forgiveness plays a central role in fostering love, trust, and understanding. It helps us navigate conflicts, repair ruptures, and create an environment of compassion and acceptance for our children and grandchildren.

Forgiveness in relationships is a transformative and liberating practice. It holds the potential to heal wounds, restore connections, and cultivate personal and spiritual growth. By embracing forgiveness, we can create a path to inner peace, harmony, and a more loving world for ourselves and future generations.

Rebuilding Trust and Healing Wounds through Forgiveness

When it comes to forgiveness in relationships, the ability to let go of past hurts and forgive both ourselves and others is essential. By embracing forgiveness, we create a space for healing and growth, allowing the relationship to flourish once again. It offers an opportunity to rebuild trust, foster empathy, and cultivate a deeper connection with our loved ones.

Forgiveness is a transformative force that has the power to rebuild trust, heal wounds, and bring about spiritual freedom and inner peace. Whether it is in personal relationships, religious and spiritual contexts, trauma healing, personal development, addiction recovery, parenting and family dynamics, the workplace, criminal justice, overcoming betrayal, or cultural and societal contexts, forgiveness holds the key to unlocking profound healing and growth.

3

Forgiveness in Religious

3 Chapter Forgiveness in Religious Spiritual Contexts

Forgiveness as a Spiritual Practice

In the journey towards spiritual freedom and inner peace, forgiveness plays a vital role. This chapter explores the power of forgiveness as a spiritual practice, addressing its significance in various aspects of life, including relationships, religious or spiritual contexts, healing trauma, self-growth, addiction recovery, parenting, family dynamics, the workplace, criminal justice, overcoming betrayal, and cultural and societal contexts.

Spirituality and forgiveness often go hand in hand. Many religious and spiritual traditions emphasize forgiveness to cultivate compassion, empathy, and love. By forgiving others and ourselves, we align with higher spiritual principles and nurture our spiritual growth.

Forgiveness is also a powerful tool in healing trauma. It enables individuals to reclaim their power, let go of victimhood, and release the pain that trauma has inflicted. By forgiving those who caused harm, individuals can break free from the cycle of suffering and move towards healing and wholeness.

Six years ago, I traveled to Renton, NJ, to visit my sister and see my son who was staying with her at the time. Accompanied by two other sisters, I arrived at her house. However, instead of receiving a warm welcome, she expressed disappointment that I hadn't called beforehand to request permission to visit. Despite explaining that my primary intention was to see my son, not her, she insisted that I leave her porch. Despite numerous attempts to apologize over the years, she has remained unwilling to accept my apology.

Some individuals may choose not to forgive, despite your sincere apology, but you can still make efforts to mend the relationship. Another time, my niece posted an angry message on Facebook, and I promptly called her to express my discontent. In response, she asserted her independence, stating she didn't require permission to post on her own page. I urged her to consider the family's reputation, which led to her becoming upset and avoiding contact with me for months, despite my subsequent apologies, which she declined to accept.

Forgiveness maybe well intended, and in some cases but may not be received as such, we still have to do our part to repair the breach. By forgiving ourselves for past mistakes and shortcomings, we allow space for growth, self-acceptance, and self-love. It is through forgiveness that we learn from our experiences and evolve into better versions of ourselves.

Bill's Journey

Once upon a time, there was a man named Bill whose childhood was marred by darkness. Growing up in a home filled with abuse, he endured pain that left scars both seen and unseen. His parents, the very people who should have provided love and protection, were instead the source of his torment. As a result, Bill grew up with walls around his heart, unable to trust or connect with others.

Despite his best efforts to bury the memories and move on, the trauma of his past haunted him, casting a shadow over every relationship he attempted to form. Trust was a luxury he couldn't afford, and forgiveness seemed like an impossible feat. How could he forgive the ones who had caused him so much pain?

It wasn't until Bill sought help through therapy that he began to confront the demons of his past. Opening up to his counselor, Sara, he finally revealed the horrors he had endured as a child. With patience and understanding, Sara gently encouraged Bill to explore the possibility of forgiveness.

At first, the idea seemed absurd to Bill. How could he possibly forgive his parents for the suffering they had inflicted upon him? But Sara persisted, guiding him through the tangled web of emotions and helping him see that forgiveness wasn't about excusing their actions; it was about freeing himself from the chains of resentment and anger that bound him.

Through years of hard work and soul-searching, Bill slowly began to let go of the bitterness that had consumed him for so long. It was a painful process, fraught with tears and moments of doubt, but with Sara's unwavering support, he found the strength to forgive his parents.

In a courageous act of reconciliation, Bill reached out to his mother and father, confronting them with his past and offering them forgiveness. The road to healing wasn't easy, and scars remained, but in forgiving his parents, Bill reclaimed his power and took the first step towards healing.

With newfound freedom in his heart, Bill opened himself up to the possibility of love. And it was in the gentle embrace of a woman named Renee that he found solace and joy. Together, they embarked on a journey of love and companionship, building a life filled with laughter and happiness.

As they welcomed three beautiful children into their lives, Bill marveled at the miracle of forgiveness. Though his past had been fraught with pain and darkness, he had emerged stronger and more resilient than ever before. And in the arms of his loving family, he found the peace and wholeness he had been searching for all along.

In conclusion, forgiveness is a transformative spiritual practice that has far-reaching effects in various aspects of life. By embracing forgiveness, individuals can experience spiritual freedom, inner peace, and profound personal growth.

The Role of Forgiveness in Various Religious and Spiritual Traditions

In our book, "Forgiveness: A Path to Spiritual Freedom and Inner Peace," we delve into the profound concept of forgiveness and explore its significance in various religions and spiritual traditions. This chapter aims to shed light on how forgiveness plays a crucial role in different aspects of life and offers guidance for individuals seeking spiritual growth and inner peace.

Forgiveness is a universal theme that transcends cultural boundaries, making it relevant to people from all walks of life. Whether you are a parent, child, grandparent, wife, or husband, the concept of forgiveness holds immense value in your personal relationships. We examine how forgiveness can mend strained relationships, heal wounds, and foster deep connections among family members. Through forgiveness, we can create harmonious dynamics within our families and build a foundation of love and understanding.

The healing power of forgiveness is another significant aspect we explore in this chapter. We discuss how forgiveness can be a transformative tool for healing emotional trauma and freeing ourselves from the burden of past hurts. By embracing forgiveness, we can release resentment, find closure, and embark on a path of emotional healing and personal growth.

4

Forgiveness in Healing Trauma

4 Chapter Forgiveness in Healing Trauma

Understanding the Connection Between Forgiveness and Trauma

Trauma is an all-too-common experience that affects individuals from all walks of life, including parents, children, grandparents, husbands, and wives. It can leave lasting emotional scars and disrupt relationships, both within families and in broader societal contexts. However, one powerful tool that can help individuals heal and find inner peace is forgiveness.

In this chapter, we will explore the profound connection between forgiveness and trauma, examining how forgiveness can be a path to spiritual freedom and inner peace.

First, let's describe Trauma. Trauma is any event that psychologically overwhelms you, often resulting in shock, denial, and changes in the body, mind, and behavior. Not the actual event, but *your* response to the event.

Trauma refers to an emotional response to a distressing or disturbing event that overwhelms an individual's ability to cope. Traumatic events can vary widely in nature and intensity, ranging from physical or emotional abuse, natural disasters, accidents, violence, or the sudden loss of a loved one, among others.

When someone experiences trauma, their sense of safety, security, and well-being is profoundly disrupted. This can lead to a range of psychological and emotional symptoms, such as flashbacks, nightmares, intrusive thoughts, hypervigilance, avoidance behaviors, anxiety, depression, and difficulty forming or maintaining relationships. Trauma can have long-lasting effects on a person's mental, emotional, and physical health if not addressed and treated appropriately.

What may evoke trauma for one person may not have the same impact on another. For instance, during my childhood, encountering loose dogs in my neighborhood while walking to school was a regular occurrence. As a result, I developed anxiety around aggressive dogs. While some of my friends may approach dogs without hesitation, I approach with caution, particularly around breeds like German Shepherds and Pit Bulls, as the memory of those past experiences still lingers in my mind.

When trauma occurs, it often engenders deep pain, anger, and resentment. These negative emotions can fester within individuals, leading to a cycle of suffering and further damaging their physical, emotional, and spiritual well-being. However, forgiveness offers a transformative solution. By choosing to forgive, individuals can begin to release the burdens of their past and find a path towards healing and personal growth.

Furthermore, forgiveness plays a vital role in healing trauma. It allows individuals to reclaim their power, release the grip of their past, and find freedom from the chains of pain and suffering.

Forgiveness from trauma likely needs professional help and guidance as the trauma becomes deep seated and well hidden. If you're supporting someone who has suffered trauma and is struggling to heal and forgive, I would advise you to seek professional help.

Seeking therapy or counseling with a qualified mental health professional who specializes in trauma. Therapy can provide a safe space for individuals to process their experiences, understand their emotions, and develop coping strategies.

Prioritize self-care activities that promote healing, such as exercise, mindfulness, journaling, spending time in nature, or engaging in hobbies they enjoy. Taking care of your physical, emotional, and mental well-being is essential on the path to recovery.

It's okay to feel a range of emotions, including anger, sadness, fear, or confusion, in response to your trauma. Your feelings about what happened to you are real and valid. You are not alone in your journey.

Recognize your boundaries and assert your needs in relationships and situations that may trigger your trauma. Be encouraged to communicate your boundaries clearly and assertively and prioritize your safety and well-being.

Forgiveness is a deeply personal process and may not happen overnight. Explore the concept of forgiveness at your own pace and in your own time. Forgiveness is not about excusing or condoning the actions of others but about releasing the hold that resentment and anger has on your life.

Acknowledge and celebrate your progress, no matter how small. Healing from trauma and forgiving others is a gradual process, and every step forward is a significant achievement worth recognizing. Above all, remember that healing and forgiveness are possible, and you deserve to live a life free from the burden of their past trauma

Healing Emotional Wounds through Forgiveness

In our journey through life, we all encounter emotional wounds that can weigh heavily on our hearts and minds. These wounds may be the result of hurtful words, actions, or betrayals that we have experienced in relationships, or trauma, Regardless of the source, the path to healing these wounds often begins with forgiveness.

Forgiveness is a transformative process that allows us to release the pain and resentment that we carry within us. It is not about condoning the hurtful actions or pretending that they never happened. Instead, it is a conscious choice to let go of the negative emotions that keep us **trapped in the past.**

In relationships, forgiveness is essential for repairing the bonds that have been damaged by conflicts or betrayals. It requires open communication, empathy, and a willingness to let go of grudges. Forgiveness allows couples to rebuild trust and create a stronger foundation for their future together.

There was once a 15-year-old girl named Renee whose mother named Alexis was a single parent while raising her in a very strict church. One day while they were preparing dinner, Alexis noticed that Renee's stomach was sticking out and discovered that Renee was pregnant. Both shocked and upset, Alexis began to severely beat Renee. Renee ran from the house to her grandmother's house, which was close by. Renee's grandmother called Social Services on her daughter Alexis. Out of shame, Renee dropped out of school and after the child was borne, the child was raised by the grandmother. After that traumatic incident, Alexis and Renee had a strained relationship for years.

The 1st incident was the pregnancy, which caused Renee to drop out of school. The 2nd was the beating by her mother, which tore their relationship to shreds. The 3rd suffered by Renee was having to surrender her child due to her inability to take child of the child.

Then there is Alexis. Alexis suffered too. Her 1st was the shock she suffered when he discovered that her 15-year-old child was pregnant. Her 2nd was her loss of control when she beat Renee. Her 3rd was the loss of the relationship with her daughter due to her reaction to Renee's pregnancy.

When you speak to both people, (yes, this is a true story) both feel that there were the victim and the other was wrong. In order for each of them to forgive, it is important to stop "finger pointing" and blaming.

To achieve forgiveness in this case, Renee should:
Renee should allow herself to fully acknowledge and process her emotions about what happened. This might involve journaling, talking to a trusted friend or therapist, or engaging in activities that help her express her feelings in a healthy way.

Renee should try to understand her mother's perspective. While it doesn't excuse her mother's actions, understanding why her mother reacted the way she did may help Renee gain empathy and perspective. This could involve having honest conversations with her mother or seeking insight from other family members who may have a different perspective on the situation.

Forgiveness doesn't mean forgetting or condoning the behavior that hurt her. Renee should establish clear boundaries with her mother to protect herself from further harm. This might involve limiting contact with her mother or establishing guidelines for their interactions.

Renee could try to put herself in her mother's shoes and consider the challenges and struggles her mother may have faced that led to her actions. Empathy can help Renee develop a more compassionate and understanding attitude towards her mother, which may facilitate the forgiveness process.

Forgiving her mother may be easier with the support of others. Renee could seek guidance from a therapist, counselor, or support group who can provide her with tools and strategies for forgiveness and healing. Additionally, leaning on friends, family members, or spiritual advisors for support can also be helpful.

Renee should focus on her own healing. Ultimately, forgiveness is a gift Renee gives herself, allowing her to let go of anger and resentment and move forward with her life. Renee should prioritize her own healing and well-being, engaging in self-care practices and activities that bring her joy and fulfillment. Same for Alexis.

Forgiveness is a process that takes time and effort. Each should be patient and understand that forgiveness may not happen overnight. It's okay to take breaks from the forgiveness process if they need to and revisit it when they feel ready.

By taking these steps, both can work towards forgiving each other and freeing their selves from the burden of anger and resentment, ultimately finding peace and healing in the process.

5

Forgiveness in Self Growth and Personal Development

5 Chapter Forgiveness in Self Growth and Personal Development

The Power of Self-Forgiveness

In our journey towards spiritual freedom and inner peace, one of the most crucial steps we must take is to learn the power of self-forgiveness. As parents, children, grandparents, husbands, and wives, we often find ourselves holding onto guilt and shame for past mistakes and shortcomings. This burden not only weighs us down but also affects our relationships, our ability to heal from trauma, and our personal growth and development.

Self-forgiveness is the act of releasing ourselves from the grip of self-blame and self-condemnation. It involves acknowledging our mistakes, taking responsibility for them, and then choosing to let go of the negative emotions associated with them. When we forgive ourselves, we open the door to healing, personal growth, and the possibility of building healthy relationships.

Not forgiving ourselves can significantly hinder one's self-development in several ways in ways that we don't realize.

Stagnation is a result of holding onto guilt and self-blame can keep us stuck in the past, preventing us from moving forward and making progress in our lives. We may dwell on past mistakes and failures, replaying them in our minds and feeling paralyzed by regret. This emotional stagnation inhibits our ability to set goals, take action, and pursue our aspirations.

Self-sabotage is what happens when we don't forgive ourselves, we may unconsciously engage in self-sabotaging behaviors as a form of punishment or self-punishment. This can manifest as procrastination, avoidance, or engaging in destructive habits that undermine our well-being and hinder our growth. By harboring feelings of guilt and shame, we may subconsciously believe that we don't deserve success or happiness, leading us to sabotage our own efforts.

Low self-esteem is a result of not forgiving ourselves can erode our self-esteem and self-worth, leading to negative self-perceptions and beliefs. We may internalize our mistakes and failures, viewing ourselves as inherently flawed or unworthy of love and acceptance. This negative self-image can undermine our confidence, resilience, and ability to pursue our goals with conviction.

Fear of failure is a result of what happens when we don't forgive ourselves for past mistakes, we may develop a fear of failure that holds us back from taking risks and embracing new opportunities. We may become overly cautious and avoidant, choosing to remain within our comfort zones rather than venture into the unknown. This fear of failure stifles our growth and prevents us from reaching our full potential.

Relationship challenges will likely occur for not forgiving ourselves, which can impact our relationships with others. Our feelings of guilt and shame may interfere with our ability to connect authentically and empathize with others. We may fear judgment or rejection, leading us to withdraw or withhold our true selves from others. Healthy relationships are essential for personal development, as they provide support, feedback, and opportunities for growth.

Not forgiving ourselves can impede our self-development by fostering emotional stagnation, self-sabotage, low self-esteem, fear of failure, and relationship challenges. By practicing self-compassion, acceptance, and forgiveness, we can release these obstacles and create space for personal growth, healing, and transformation.

On the other *Unforgiveness* can significantly impede self-development in several ways as described below.

Emotional stagnation will result due to holding onto unforgiveness can keep us trapped in negative emotions such as anger, resentment, and bitterness. These emotions consume our mental and emotional energy, leaving little room for growth and self-improvement. Instead of focusing on personal development, we may find ourselves stuck in a cycle of rumination and negativity.

Limited perspective will result due to unforgiveness, which often arises from a sense of injustice or hurt inflicted by others. By holding onto grudges, we may become fixated on the perceived wrongs done to us, which can narrow our perspective and prevent us from seeing the bigger picture. This limited viewpoint inhibits our ability to empathize with others, understand different perspectives, and cultivate meaningful relationships—all of which are essential for personal growth and development.

Interpersonal barriers will be impacted due to unforgiveness creating barriers in our relationships with others. It can lead to conflicts, misunderstandings, and breakdowns in communication, hindering our ability to form and maintain healthy connections. Healthy relationships are crucial for personal development, as they provide support, feedback, and opportunities for growth.

Self-limiting beliefs due to holding onto unforgiveness, which can reinforce negative self-beliefs and undermine our self-esteem. We may internalize the idea that we are victims or that we are unworthy of forgiveness ourselves. These self-limiting beliefs can sabotage our efforts to pursue our goals, take risks, and step outside of our comfort zones—all of which are necessary for personal development and growth.

Physical health impacted, due to unforgiveness linked to negative physical health outcomes, including increased stress, elevated blood pressure, and weakened immune function. Chronic stress and negative emotions associated with unforgiveness can take a toll on our overall well-being, making it difficult to focus on self-care activities that support physical health and vitality.

As a barrier to self-development, unforgiveness acts as an impediment by perpetuating negative emotions, limiting our perspective, creating interpersonal barriers, reinforcing self-limiting beliefs, and undermining our physical health. By practicing forgiveness, we can release these obstacles and create space for personal growth, healing, and transformation.

Using Forgiveness as a Tool for Personal Transformation.

Forgiveness in relationships is a vital component that allows individuals to mend broken bonds and restore harmony. By embracing forgiveness, we can transcend conflicts and cultivate healthier and more fulfilling connections with our loved ones.

Forgiveness is essential for personal growth, both of oneself and others, is crucial for personal development. Holding onto grudges, resentment, and self-blame inhibits our ability to move forward, make progress, and reach our full potential.

Self-forgiveness is foundational, laying the groundwork for self-development. When we forgive ourselves for past mistakes and shortcomings, we release the burdens of guilt and shame that hold us back, allowing us to embrace new opportunities and pursue our goals with confidence.

Forgiveness fosters resilience, cultivating resilience by helping us bounce back from setbacks and challenges. When we forgive ourselves and others, we build emotional strength and fortitude, enabling us to navigate life's ups and downs with greater ease and grace.

Forgiveness promotes healthy relationships, which is essential for building and maintaining healthy relationships. By practicing forgiveness, we foster empathy, understanding, and compassion towards ourselves and others, creating deeper connections and stronger bonds.

Self-development requires self-compassion, that is fueled by self-compassion, acceptance, and self-love. When we treat ourselves with kindness and understanding, we create an environment that nurtures growth, resilience, and well-being.

Forgiveness is a continuous process, may take time. This ordeal is not a one-time event but an ongoing process. It requires patience, perseverance, and commitment to let go of past hurts and embrace a mindset of forgiveness and healing.

Forgiveness of oneself and others is integral to self-development. By practicing forgiveness, cultivating self-compassion, and embracing a mindset of growth and resilience, we create the conditions for personal transformation and fulfillment.

6

Forgiveness in Addition Recovery

6 Chapter Forgiveness in Addition Recovery

The Role of Forgiveness in Overcoming Addiction

Addiction is a complex and devastating issue that affects not only the individual struggling with it but also their loved ones. It can tear families apart, strain relationships, and cause profound pain and suffering. However, one powerful tool that can aid in the recovery process is forgiveness. In this chapter, we will explore the role of forgiveness in overcoming addiction and how it can bring about spiritual freedom and inner peace.

In the realm of addiction recovery, forgiveness is instrumental in breaking the cycle of guilt and shame. By forgiving oneself for past mistakes and embracing a mindset of self-compassion, individuals can let go of the self-destructive behaviors that perpetuate addiction and instead focus on self-care and healing. Forgiveness is an essential component of the addiction recovery process. It allows individuals to release emotional burdens, repair relationships, and find spiritual freedom and inner peace.

Forgiving Oneself and Others in the Journey to Recovery

In addiction recovery, forgiveness is a vital step towards healing and sobriety. It involves forgiving ourselves for past actions and forgiving others who may have contributed to our addiction. Through forgiveness, we can break free from the shame and guilt that often accompany addiction and find the strength to move forward.

Begin TODAY to repair the breach between yourself and your family.

Forgiving oneself for struggling with addiction can be a challenging journey, but it's an essential step toward healing and recovery.

Acknowledge the addiction by recognizing that addiction is a complex issue. Addiction is not a reflection of your worth as a person. Acceptance of the problem is the first step toward forgiveness. Seek Support by surrounding yourself with supportive people who understand addiction and its challenges. This could include friends, family, support groups, or a therapist.

Educate Yourself by reading about addiction and its effects. Learn about addiction, its causes, and its effects on the brain and behavior. Understanding the science behind addiction can help you realize that it's a medical condition, not a moral failing.

Take Responsibility for your actions. While it's important to recognize that addiction is a disease, taking responsibility for your actions and their consequences is also crucial. This doesn't mean blaming yourself, but rather acknowledging the role you played and committing to making positive changes.

Practice Self-Compassion. Be kind to yourself. Treat yourself with kindness and understanding. Understand that addiction is a struggle, and it's okay to have setbacks along the way. Practice self-care activities that promote physical, emotional, and mental well-being.

Forgive Yourself for your past. Recognize that everyone makes mistakes, and that forgiveness is a process. It may not happen overnight, but with time and effort, you can learn to let go of guilt and shame. Make Amends to those you have harmed. If your addiction has harmed others, consider making amends where possible. This could involve apologizing, making restitution, or taking steps to repair damaged relationships.

Focus on your recovery and avoid judging others in the process. Shift your focus from dwelling on past mistakes to working toward a brighter future. Engage in activities that support your recovery, such as attending therapy, participating in support groups, and practicing healthy coping strategies.

Set Realistic Goals, take baby steps. Break your recovery journey into manageable steps and set realistic goals for yourself. Celebrate your achievements, no matter how small, and be patient with yourself as you progress.

Stay Connected to your support network, friends, and family. On the other hand, stay away from friends who used to share your drug habit. Stay connected to your network and continue to seek help when needed. Recovery is an ongoing process and having a strong support system can help you navigate the ups and downs.

Forgiving yourself is a process that takes time and effort, but it's an important step toward healing and moving forward in your recovery journey. Remember, you are worth this journey.

7

Forgiveness in Parenting and Family Dynamics

7 Chapter Forgiveness in Parenting and Family Dynamics

Teaching Forgiveness to Children

Forgiveness is a powerful tool that can bring about spiritual freedom and inner peace. It is a skill that can transform relationships, heal trauma, foster personal growth, and even aid in addiction recovery. In our fast-paced and often chaotic world, it is essential to equip our children with the ability to forgive, as it will serve them in every aspect of their lives.

Forgiveness in parenting and family dynamics is particularly crucial. As parents, we have the responsibility to guide our children towards emotional intelligence and empathy. Teaching forgiveness at a young age can help children understand that everyone makes mistakes and that holding onto grudges only leads to bitterness and resentment. By encouraging forgiveness, we create an environment where conflicts are resolved peacefully, and love and understanding thrive.

Teaching forgiveness to children is essential for their personal growth and the betterment of society. By instilling this value in their hearts and minds, we equip them with a tool that will serve them in their relationships, personal development, and various social contexts. As parents, grandparents, spouses, and individuals, we have the power to shape a world where forgiveness is embraced, healing is sought, and peace is attained.

Healing Family Wounds through Forgiveness

In the complex tapestry of family dynamics, wounds are bound to occur. Hurtful words, misunderstandings, and past traumas can strain relationships, causing deep emotional pain and resentment. However, there is a powerful antidote that can mend these fractures and restore harmony within the family unit: forgiveness.

Will's Journey

Once there lived a man named Will, who admired his father Justin, a doctor, greatly. His mother excelled as a lawyer, and his sister found success in acting. However, Will harbored bitterness and resentment towards his family due to his perceived lack of success. His parents' constant comparisons to his sister, with remarks like "we wish you were more like your sister," fueled his resentment, leading him to blame them for his own failures.

How can Will move past his hurt feelings and forgive his family?

Forgiving family members for past hurts and overcoming feelings of bitterness and resentment can be a challenging process, but it's achievable with dedication and effort. Will should recognize and accept his feelings of bitterness and resentment toward his family. It's important for him to acknowledge these emotions without judgment.

Confront the situation head on, by identifying the triggers, specific events or situations that trigger his negative feelings toward his family.

By understanding what triggers his emotions, Will can develop coping strategies to manage them.

By practicing empathy with family members' perspectives and motivations, it is likely that Will's parents' will realize that their comparison were not successful in motivating him. They were misguided attempts to motivate him, rather than intentional acts of cruelty. Empathizing with their intentions can help him let go of resentment.

Will should try to have open and honest communications conversations with his family members about how their actions have affected him, by expressing his feelings in a constructive manner can foster understanding and lead to resolution. If certain interactions with his family members consistently lead to negative emotions, Will should establish boundaries to protect his mental and emotional well-being. This could involve limiting contact or setting clear expectations for behavior.

Will needs to have a mental paradigm shift to shift his focus from blaming his family for his perceived failures to taking responsibility for his own growth and development. Setting personal goals and pursuing his passions can help him build confidence and a sense of fulfillment independent of his family's expectations.

Working with a therapist can provide Will with support and guidance as he navigates his feelings toward his family. A therapist can help him explore underlying issues, develop coping strategies, and learn techniques for forgiveness and emotional healing. Forgiveness is a process that takes time and effort. Will practice forgiveness by letting go of grudges, releasing negative emotions, and choosing to focus on the present rather than dwelling on the past.

He can demonstrate gratitude by focusing on the positive aspects of his relationships with his family members and the ways in which they have supported him. Recognizing and appreciating the good can help counteract feelings of bitterness and resentment.

Will can find moral support with friends, mentors, or support groups who can provide him with encouragement and validation as he works through his feelings toward his family. By taking these steps, Will can begin the journey toward forgiveness and healing, ultimately freeing himself from the burden of bitterness and resentment toward his family. By letting go of past hurts, Will and his family members can build stronger connections based on trust, compassion, and acceptance.

8

Forgiveness in the Workplace

8 Chapter Forgiveness in the Workplace

Creating a Forgiving Culture in the Workplace

In today's fast-paced and competitive world, the workplace can often be a breeding ground for stress, conflict, and resentment. However, fostering a forgiving culture within the workplace is crucial for the well-being and success of both individuals and organizations. This chapter explores the importance of forgiveness in the workplace and offers practical strategies for creating a forgiving culture.

Forgiveness in the workplace is essential because it promotes healthier relationships, improves productivity, and enhances overall job satisfaction. When conflicts arise, holding grudges and harboring resentment only hinders collaboration and teamwork. By embracing forgiveness, individuals can let go of past grievances and focus on finding solutions and moving forward together.

To create a forgiving culture in the workplace, it is important to cultivate open communication and encourage dialogue. Providing a safe space for employees to express their concerns, share their perspectives, and resolve conflicts is vital. This can be achieved through team-building exercises, conflict resolution workshops, and regular check-ins to address any underlying issues.

Additionally, fostering empathy and understanding among employees can contribute to a forgiving culture. Encouraging individuals to put themselves in others' shoes can help them see things from different perspectives and develop compassion. This can be achieved through training programs that focus on emotional intelligence, active listening, and empathy-building exercises.

Promoting forgiveness in the workplace also involves setting clear expectations and boundaries. Encouraging individuals to take responsibility for their actions and holding them accountable for any harm caused is crucial. However, it is equally important to provide opportunities for growth, learning, and redemption. By offering forgiveness and second chances, individuals can feel supported and motivated to improve their behavior.

Furthermore, leaders play a pivotal role in creating a forgiving culture. Leading by example and demonstrating forgiveness in their own actions and interactions can inspire others to do the same. Leaders should also provide guidance and support to employees, ensuring that forgiveness is seen as a strength rather than a weakness.

Creating a forgiving culture in the workplace is essential for fostering healthy relationships, improving productivity, and enhancing overall job satisfaction. By cultivating open communication, empathy, and understanding, setting clear expectations and boundaries, and providing leadership support, organizations can create an environment where forgiveness thrives.

Forgiving Colleagues and Resolving Workplace Conflicts

In the hustle and bustle of our everyday lives, conflicts are bound to arise, especially in the workplace. Whether it's a disagreement with a colleague, a clash of personalities, or a misunderstanding that escalates into a full-blown conflict, these situations can be incredibly challenging and stressful. However, forgiveness offers a powerful tool for finding resolution, fostering harmony, and promoting personal and professional growth.

Jose's Journey

Jose caught wind of some office gossip while passing through the breakroom, only to find a sudden hush upon his arrival. Annoyed, he confronted Sheila once the room cleared, seeking clarification on what was said. Sheila disclosed that his colleagues had remarked on his alleged offensive body odor, attributing it to his cultural culinary practices involving heavy use of pepper. Jose, incensed, defended himself, attributing the scent to his cultural habits.

The following day, his entrance prompted laughter from his co-workers, further infuriating him. His outburst led to intervention from the supervisor, who advised him to manage his emotions and hygiene better. Following the incident, Jose withdrew from office interactions, confining communication solely to his supervisor.

What steps does Jose take to forgive his coworkers?

Reflection on what happened and his reaction. Jose might first reflect on his own actions and reactions in the situation. This could involve considering whether his initial response was warranted and if there were better ways to handle the situation.

Jose could try to understand his coworkers' perspective. He might consider their cultural backgrounds, personalities, and the context in which they made the comments. Understanding that they might not have intended to hurt him personally could help him empathize with them.

He could initiate a conversation with his coworkers, individually or as a group, to address the issue. He could express how their comments made him feel and clarify any misunderstandings. Open communication could help clear the air and rebuild trust among them.

Forgiveness is a personal choice, and Jose might need to consciously decide to let go of any resentment or anger he holds towards his coworkers. This doesn't mean he has to forget what happened, but rather that he chooses not to let it negatively affect his relationships with them.

Once forgiveness is granted, Jose can focus on rebuilding his relationships with his coworkers. This might involve actively participating in office activities, engaging in small talk, and showing willingness to collaborate with them professionally.

While forgiving his coworkers, Jose should also ensure that boundaries are set to prevent similar situations from occurring in the future. This could involve communicating his expectations regarding respectful behavior and addressing any issues promptly if they arise again.

By taking these steps, Jose can work towards forgiving his coworkers and fostering a more positive and harmonious work environment. Forgiveness is a powerful tool for resolving workplace conflicts and fostering healthy relationships. By practicing forgiveness, we can create a harmonious work environment, enhance productivity, and promote personal and professional growth. Whether it is forgiving our colleagues, ourselves, or seeking forgiveness from others, this practice is crucial for building strong and fulfilling relationships in the workplace. Let forgiveness be the guiding principle in all our interactions, enabling us to navigate conflicts with grace and compassion.

9

Forgiveness in Criminal Justice and Restorative Justice Practices

9 Chapter Forgiveness in Criminal Justice and Restorative Justice Practices

The Power of Forgiveness in Restorative Justice

In the realm of criminal justice and restorative practices, forgiveness represents a transformative force that extends far beyond the traditional concepts of punishment and retribution. Instead of solely focusing on meting out consequences for wrongdoing, forgiveness introduces the concept of healing and reconciliation into the equation.

Firstly, forgiveness acknowledges the humanity of both the offender and the victim. It recognizes that individuals can make mistakes, but those mistakes do not define their entire being. By extending forgiveness, victims reclaim agency over their own lives, refusing to be defined solely by the harm inflicted upon them. Similarly, offenders are given the opportunity to confront their actions, take responsibility, and seek redemption.

Moreover, forgiveness facilitates healing on both individual and communal levels. For victims, it can provide a sense of closure and release from the burden of resentment and anger. By letting go of negative emotions, victims can begin the process of healing and moving forward with their lives. Similarly, offenders may experience profound transformation through the act of seeking forgiveness and making amends. This process not only promotes personal growth but also fosters a sense of accountability and empathy.

Furthermore, forgiveness has the power to restore broken relationships and rebuild trust within communities. Restorative justice practices often emphasize dialogue and reconciliation between victims and offenders, allowing both parties to share their experiences, express remorse, and seek understanding. Through this process, individuals can confront the harm caused by crime and work together towards repairing the social fabric that has been damaged.

In essence, forgiveness represents a paradigm shift in the criminal justice system, one that prioritizes healing and reconciliation over punishment and revenge. By embracing forgiveness as a central tenet of restorative practices, societies can move towards a more compassionate and inclusive approach to justice, one that seeks to repair the harm caused by crime and promote the well-being of all individuals involved.

Healing and Transforming Lives through Forgiveness in the Criminal Justice System

Forgiveness plays a significant role in the criminal justice system, particularly within the framework of restorative justice. In restorative justice practices, forgiveness often serves as a cornerstone for victim-offender reconciliation. Through facilitated dialogues and mediation, victims have the opportunity to express their pain and anger directly to the offender, while offenders can take responsibility for their actions and seek forgiveness. This process can lead to healing for both parties and promote a sense of closure that traditional punitive measures may not achieve.

Forgiveness contributes to the healing and restoration of individuals affected by crime. Victims who can forgive may experience emotional relief and a sense of empowerment over their own lives. Similarly, offenders who receive forgiveness may be motivated to make amends and reintegrate into society as productive members. This focus on healing and restoration aligns with the goals of rehabilitation within the criminal justice system.

Research suggests that restorative justice approaches, which emphasize forgiveness and reconciliation, can contribute to lower rates of recidivism compared to traditional punitive measures. By addressing the underlying causes of criminal behavior and promoting empathy and accountability, restorative practices may help break the cycle of reoffending.

Forgiveness extends beyond individual interactions to encompass broader community healing. When victims forgive offenders and offenders seek forgiveness, it can foster a sense of solidarity and interconnectedness within communities affected by crime. This collective healing process strengthens social bonds and promotes a sense of trust and safety among community members.

Forgiveness challenges the traditional notion of justice as solely punitive and retributive. Instead, it introduces a more compassionate and humanizing approach to addressing harm and wrongdoing. By balancing accountability with opportunities for redemption and reconciliation, forgiveness enriches the concept of justice and promotes a more holistic understanding of the needs of all stakeholders involved.

Forgiveness intersects with various aspects of the criminal justice system, offering alternative pathways to address harm, promote healing, and restore relationships within communities affected by crime. Incorporating forgiveness into criminal justice practices can lead to more equitable and compassionate outcomes for victims, offenders, and society as a whole.

The Wrongfully Convicted:

Here are a few examples of individuals who were wrongly convicted.

Anthony Ray Hinton spent 30 years on death row in Alabama for crimes he did not commit. He was wrongfully convicted of two murders based on flawed forensic evidence. In 2015, he was exonerated and released from prison. Alabama later passed a law providing compensation for those wrongfully convicted, and Hinton received financial compensation for his wrongful imprisonment.

Darryl Hunt was wrongfully convicted of the rape and murder of a newspaper editor in North Carolina in 1984. He spent nearly 19 years in prison before DNA evidence exonerated him in 2004. Following his release, Hunt received compensation from the state of North Carolina for his wrongful conviction and imprisonment.

Ronald Cotton was wrongfully convicted of rape in North Carolina in 1984 based on mistaken eyewitness identification. He served over 10 years in prison before DNA evidence cleared him of the crime in 1995. Following his exoneration, Cotton received compensation from the state of North Carolina for the years he spent wrongfully incarcerated.

Ryan Ferguson was wrongfully convicted of murder in Missouri in 2005 based on coerced witness testimony. He spent nearly 10 years in prison before his conviction was overturned in 2013 due to the discovery of new evidence. Ferguson later received compensation from the state of Missouri for his wrongful imprisonment.

These cases highlight the profound injustices that can occur within the criminal justice system and the importance of providing compensation to individuals who have been wrongfully convicted and imprisoned for crimes they did not commit. While financial compensation cannot fully restore the years lost to wrongful incarceration, it can help support individuals as they rebuild their lives after exoneration.

How can the "Wrongfully Convicted" Forgive?

Forgiving those who prosecuted and sent them to prison can be an incredibly challenging and deeply personal process for individuals who have been wrongfully convicted.

Wrongfully convicted individuals may strive to understand the circumstances that led to their prosecution and imprisonment. This could involve recognizing systemic flaws within the criminal justice system, such as flawed forensic evidence, biased witness testimony, or prosecutorial misconduct. By understanding the broader context in which their wrongful conviction occurred, they may find it easier to empathize with those involved in their prosecution.

Forgiveness does not necessarily mean condoning or excusing the actions of those who prosecuted them. Instead, wrongfully convicted individuals may choose to separate the act of prosecution from the individuals responsible for it. They may recognize that prosecutors were acting within the confines of their roles and duties, even if their actions resulted in unjust consequences.

Some wrongfully convicted individuals may cultivate empathy for those who prosecuted them, recognizing that they too may have been influenced by societal pressures, personal biases, or the desire for justice. By acknowledging the humanity of those involved in their prosecution, they may find it easier to extend forgiveness.

Forgiveness can be a powerful tool for personal healing and growth. Wrongfully convicted individuals may choose to forgive prosecutors as part of their own journey towards emotional and psychological well-being. By releasing feelings of anger, resentment, and bitterness, they can free themselves from the emotional burden of their wrongful conviction and move forward with their lives.

Some wrongfully convicted individuals may advocate for restorative justice practices that promote accountability, reconciliation, and healing for all parties involved. By actively engaging in dialogue with prosecutors and other stakeholders, they may seek to address the harm caused by their wrongful conviction and work towards repairing broken relationships within their communities.

Ultimately, forgiveness is a deeply personal and individual process that may unfold over time. While some wrongfully convicted individuals may find it possible to forgive those who prosecuted them, others may struggle with feelings of anger and betrayal for years to come. Regardless of the path they choose, what matters most is that they find a sense of peace and closure that allows them to move forward with their lives.

10

Forgiveness in Overcoming Betrayal

10 Chapter Forgiveness in Overcoming Betrayal

Finding Inner Peace and Freedom from Betrayal through Forgiveness

In our journey through life, we all encounter moments of betrayal - whether it is by a loved one, a friend, a colleague, or even society as a whole. The pain and anguish caused by betrayal can be overwhelming, leaving us feeling lost, hurt, and seeking solace. However, there is a path to healing, inner peace, and freedom - forgiveness.

Forgiveness is a powerful tool that can transform our lives and free us from the shackles of betrayal. It is not about condoning the actions of those who have wronged us, but rather about liberating ourselves from the burden of anger, resentment, and bitterness. By choosing forgiveness, we take back control of our own lives and emotions.

In the context of relationships, forgiveness plays a vital role in rebuilding trust and strengthening the bond between individuals. It allows for healing and growth, both personally and within the relationship itself. Whether it is a spouse, a child, a parent, or a grandparent, forgiveness can help mend broken hearts and restore harmony in family dynamics.

Rebuilding Trust and Relationships after Betrayal

Betrayal can be one of the most devastating experiences one can endure. It shatters trust, breaks relationships, and leaves lasting emotional scars.

Betrayal occurs when someone violates the trust or confidence placed in them by another person. It can take many forms, from lying and deceit to infidelity and disloyalty. Betrayal often leads to feelings of hurt, anger, and disillusionment, and recovering from it can be a challenging process.

To recover from betrayal, it's important to acknowledge and validate your feelings, accepting the range of emotions that come with betrayal, such as sadness, anger, and mistrust. Allow yourself to feel these emotions without judgment and acknowledge that they are a natural response to being betrayed.

Get it out your soul. Talking about your feelings with trusted friends, family members, or a therapist can provide validation and support during the recovery process. Sharing your experience with others can help you gain perspective, process your emotions, and feel less alone in your journey.

After experiencing betrayal, it's crucial to establish clear boundaries to protect yourself from further harm. This may involve limiting contact with the person who betrayed you, setting boundaries around what behaviors are acceptable, and prioritizing your own well-being.

Be kind and gentle with yourself as you navigate the aftermath of betrayal. Practice self-care activities that promote emotional healing, such as mindfulness, journaling, exercise, or spending time with loved ones who uplift and support you.

Rebuilding trust after betrayal takes time and effort from both parties involved. If the relationship is salvageable and both parties are willing to work on rebuilding trust, open and honest communication, consistency, and accountability are key. However, it's also important to recognize when a relationship is no longer healthy or viable and to prioritize your own well-being.

Recovering from betrayal is a complex and individual journey, and it's important to be patient and compassionate with yourself as you navigate the process. With time, self-reflection, and support from others, it is possible to heal from betrayal and move forward with greater resilience and strength.

Jane's Journey

On Valentine's Day, Jane and Bob were seated at a restaurant, commemorating the occasion. As Bob knew too well after being married to Jane for 18 years, it was also Jane's birthday. Throughout the evening,

Jane was filled with anticipation, chatting happily with her husband, envisioning a thoughtful birthday surprise at the meal's conclusion. However, her joy quickly turned to devastation when, just after they finished dining, Bob confessed that he had been involved with someone else for the past six months and expressed his desire for a divorce. Jane was left reeling, feeling utterly blindsided and betrayed on what should have been a day of celebration and love. Bob and Jane have a 17-year-old son together, so Jane knows that she will still have to be in contact with Bob.

How does Jane forgive Bob?

It's suggested for Jane to stay away from Bob until such a time that she can let go of her negative feelings. Ultimately, forgiveness is about letting go of resentment and the desire for revenge. It's a choice to release the negative emotions that weigh us down and move forward with a sense of peace and closure. Forgiveness is a deeply personal journey and can take time.

Once Jane can face Bob, she should acknowledge her feelings of hurt, betrayal, and anger. It's important for her to process these emotions rather than suppress them. Jane should try to understand why Bob made the choices he did. This doesn't mean justifying his actions, but rather gaining insight into his perspective and the circumstances that led to his betrayal.

Open and honest communication between Jane and Bob is crucial. Bob needs to express genuine remorse for his actions, take responsibility for the hurt he caused, and show a sincere commitment to rebuilding trust.

Jane may need to establish clear boundaries to protect herself emotionally. These boundaries might include seeking counseling together or individually, taking a break from the relationship to heal, or establishing guidelines for rebuilding trust.

Jane should also reflect on her own role in the relationship and any patterns that may have contributed to its breakdown. Self-awareness can help her grow and make healthier choices in the future. Forgiveness doesn't mean forgetting or instantly trusting again. It's a gradual process of rebuilding trust through consistent actions and efforts from both parties. Bob must demonstrate over time that he is trustworthy and committed to rebuilding their relationship.

It's important for Jane to remember that forgiveness is not about excusing or minimizing what Bob did but rather about freeing herself from the burden of anger and resentment. Whether she chooses to forgive Bob or not, the most important thing is for her to prioritize her own emotional well-being and make decisions that are right for her.

Forgiveness is a deeply personal process that can help release the grip of resentment and anger that betrayal can bring. Forgiveness does not mean condoning or excusing the betrayal; rather, it involves letting go of negative emotions and freeing yourself from the burden of carrying grudges. Forgiveness can be a gradual process and may not happen overnight, but it can ultimately lead to greater emotional freedom and healing.

11

Forgiveness in Cultural and Societal Contexts

11 Chapter Forgiveness in Cultural and Societal Contexts

The Role of Forgiveness in Cultural Healing and Reconciliation

Cultural healing and reconciliation are essential for building harmonious societies and fostering positive relationships among individuals from diverse backgrounds. Forgiveness plays a pivotal role in this process by allowing individuals to let go of past grievances and embrace a future of understanding, empathy, and acceptance. By forgiving, we create space for dialogue, empathy, and healing, thus transforming conflicts and bridging cultural divides.

This type of healing is aimed at addressing historical injustices, traumas, and divisions within a society by drawing upon cultural traditions, practices, and values. These concepts recognize that many societal conflicts and traumas are deeply rooted in historical injustices, colonization, oppression, and cultural genocide.

Cultural healing involves restoring and revitalizing cultural practices, languages, and traditions that have been suppressed or lost due to colonization or other forms of cultural violence. It emphasizes the importance of reconnecting individuals and communities with their cultural heritage as a means of healing from intergenerational trauma and reclaiming a sense of identity and belonging.

Reconciliation, on the other hand, involves acknowledging past wrongs, fostering understanding between different groups, and working towards healing and rebuilding relationships based on principles of justice, equality, and mutual respect. It requires addressing systemic inequalities, promoting dialogue and empathy, and actively challenging discriminatory attitudes and behaviors.

Truth-telling involves acknowledging and confronting the truth of past injustices and traumas, including the experiences of marginalized and oppressed communities.

Restorative Justice, which seeks to repair the harm caused by historical injustices through processes that prioritize healing, accountability, and community involvement rather than punitive measures. Cultural Revitalization's aim is to support efforts to preserve and revitalize indigenous languages, traditions, and knowledge systems that have been endangered or marginalized.

Community Empowerment is empowering communities to define their own paths to healing and reconciliation, based on their cultural values, needs, and priorities. Intercultural Dialogue fosters dialogue and understanding between different cultural, ethnic, and social groups to promote empathy, reconciliation, and social cohesion.

Policy reform addresses systemic inequalities and injustices through policy reforms that promote social justice, equality, and inclusion.

Cultural healing and reconciliation are ongoing processes that require commitment, patience, and collaboration from all members of society. They offer pathways towards healing collective traumas, promoting social cohesion, and building more inclusive and equitable societies.

Indian Reservations and the COVID-19 pandemic

In the aftermath of the COVID-19 pandemic, the United States government took various measures to support Indian reservations and tribal communities, recognizing the disproportionate impact of the pandemic on these populations.

The U.S. government allocated funding specifically for tribes and tribal organizations to address the health, economic, and social impacts of the pandemic. This funding included direct appropriations, grants, and support through programs such as the Coronavirus Aid, Relief, and Economic Security (CARES) Act and subsequent relief packages.

The Indian Health Service (IHS), an agency within the U.S. Department of Health and Human Services responsible for providing healthcare to Native Americans, received additional resources to support COVID-19 testing, treatment, and vaccination efforts in Indian Country. This included funding for personal protective equipment (PPE), medical supplies, and healthcare facilities.

The U.S. government worked with tribal governments and health-care providers to distribute COVID-19 vaccines to tribal communities, prioritizing access for Native Americans living on reservations. Vaccination clinics were set up in tribal communities, and outreach efforts were conducted to address vaccine hesitancy and ensure equitable access to vaccines.

Tribal governments and businesses received financial assistance through programs such as the Paycheck Protection Program (PPP) and Economic Injury Disaster Loans (EIDL) to mitigate the economic impact of the pandemic. These programs provided loans, grants, and other forms of support to help tribes maintain essential services, support businesses, and preserve jobs.

The U.S. government provided emergency food assistance to tribal communities facing food insecurity as a result of the pandemic. This included support for food distribution programs, nutrition assistance, and partnerships with tribal organizations and food banks to address hunger and food shortages.

Efforts were made to address housing and homelessness issues exacerbated by the pandemic, including funding for emergency shelter, rental assistance, and housing infrastructure improvements in tribal communities.

The U.S. Department of Education provided support for remote learning and technology access for Native American students attending schools on reservations. This included funding for internet connectivity, devices, and educational resources to support distance learning during school closures.

These efforts aimed to provide immediate relief and long-term support to tribal communities affected by the COVID-19 pandemic, recognizing the unique challenges and vulnerabilities faced by Native Americans living on reservations.

How can Native American Reservations forgive the US Government for neglecting them in the past?

Forgiveness between Indian reservations and the U.S. government for past neglect is a complex and multifaceted process that involves acknowledgment of historical injustices, healing intergenerational trauma, and fostering reconciliation and understanding. While forgiveness is ultimately a personal and collective decision, there are several steps that both parties can take to move towards reconciliation:

Acknowledgment of Past Wrongs by both parties. The U.S. government can acknowledge and take responsibility for historical injustices, including policies of forced removal, assimilation, and neglect that have disproportionately affected Native American communities. This acknowledgment validates the experiences of those who have been harmed and lays the foundation for reconciliation.

A sincere apology from the U.S. government for past wrongs can be a crucial step towards healing and reconciliation. In addition to apology, reparations, or compensation for past harms, such as funding for infrastructure development, healthcare, education, and economic development, can demonstrate a commitment to addressing the legacy of neglect and supporting the well-being of Native American communities.

Establishing truth and reconciliation commissions or similar mechanisms can provide a forum for dialogue, storytelling, and healing between Native American communities and the U.S. government. These commissions can facilitate the sharing of experiences, the uncovering of historical truths, and the promotion of understanding and empathy.

Supporting efforts to revitalize and preserve indigenous languages, cultures, and traditions can help Native American communities reclaim their identity and strengthen their resilience in the face of historical trauma. This may involve funding for cultural programs, language revitalization initiatives, and support for traditional practices and knowledge systems.

Building collaborative partnerships and engaging in meaningful consultation and decision-making with tribal governments and communities can help foster trust and mutual respect. This includes involving Native American representatives in policy-making processes, resource allocation, and initiatives that affect their communities.

Promoting education and awareness about Native American history, culture, and contemporary issues can help challenge stereotypes, dismantle misconceptions, and promote greater understanding and solidarity between Native American communities and the broader society.

Investing in programs and services that support healing, trauma recovery, and community well-being can help address the intergenerational impacts of historical trauma and neglect. This may include mental health services, cultural healing programs, and support for community-led initiatives focused on healing and reconciliation.

Ultimately, forgiveness and reconciliation are ongoing processes that require commitment, empathy, and a willingness to listen and learn from one another. By taking concrete steps towards acknowledging past wrongs, promoting healing and empowerment, and building collaborative partnerships, Indian reservations and the U.S. government can work towards a more just and equitable future.

12

Forgiveness Can Be Liberating

The Process of Forgiveness can be incredibly liberating and beneficial for both the forgiver and the forgiven. The process can release the negative emotions that weigh you down, such as anger, resentment, and bitterness, leading to emotional healing and inner peace. Holding onto grudges keeps you anchored to the past. Forgiving allows you to let go and move forward with your life. Forgiveness can mend broken relationships by fostering understanding, empathy, and reconciliation. Forgiving someone can be an opportunity for personal growth and maturity. It requires empathy, compassion, and strength.

Holding onto anger and resentment can have detrimental effects on your physical health. Forgiveness has been linked to reduced stress levels, lower blood pressure, and improved overall health. Many spiritual and religious traditions advocate forgiveness as a path to spiritual growth and enlightenment.

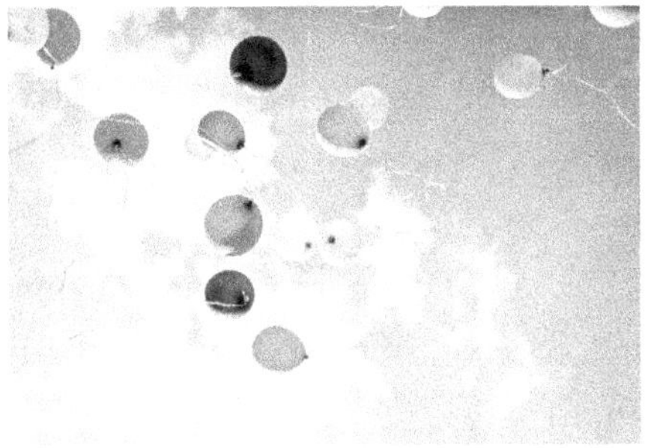

By forgiving, you can break the cycle of hurt and retaliation, promoting a more positive and compassionate way of interacting with others. Forgiveness can be empowering because it allows you to take control of your own emotions and reactions, rather than letting past events dictate your present and future.

The Bible contains numerous scriptures that emphasize the importance of forgiveness.

Matthew 6:14-15 (NIV): "For if you forgive other people when they sin against you, your heavenly Father will also forgive you. But if you do not forgive others their sins, your father will not forgive your sins."
Ephesians 4:32 (NIV): "Be kind and compassionate to one another, forgiving each other, just as in Christ God forgave you."

Colossians 3:13 (NIV): "Bear with each other and forgive one another if any of you has a grievance against someone. Forgive as the Lord forgave you."

Matthew 18:21-22 (NIV): "Then Peter came to Jesus and asked, 'Lord, how many times shall I forgive my brother or sister who sins against me? Up to seven times?' Jesus answered, 'I tell you, not seven times, but seventy-seven times.'"

Luke 6:37 (NIV): "Do not judge, and you will not be judged. Do not condemn, and you will not be condemned. Forgive, and you will be forgiven."

Mark 11:25 (NIV): "And when you stand praying, if you hold anything against anyone, forgive them, so that your Father in heaven may forgive you your sins."

James 5:16 (NIV): "Therefore confess your sins to each other and pray for each other so that you may be healed. The prayer of a righteous person is powerful and effective."

These passages highlight the importance of forgiveness in the Christian faith, emphasizing not only the act of forgiving others but also the understanding that forgiveness is tied to one's own forgiveness by God.

Forgiving others can boost your self-esteem by demonstrating your ability to rise above the pain and choose compassion and understanding. Ultimately, forgiveness can bring peace of mind. It frees you from the burden of carrying grudges and allows you to focus your energy on more positive aspects of life.

Forgiveness can have profound effects on the mind and soul as it allows one to release the negative emotions that can weigh heavily on the soul, such as anger, resentment, and bitterness. By letting go of these emotions, forgiveness opens the door to emotional healing and inner peace.

Forgiving others requires understanding their humanity and acknowledging that everyone makes mistakes. This fosters compassion and empathy, qualities that are enriching to the soul.

Forgiveness can mend broken relationships by promoting reconciliation and understanding. By letting go of grudges, you can create space for healthier, more positive connections with others. Letting go involves introspection and self-reflection. It allows you to examine your own actions and reactions, leading to greater self-awareness and personal growth.

Holding onto anger and resentment can disturb your inner peace. Forgiveness, on the other hand, brings a sense of tranquility and harmony to the soul, allowing you to live with greater serenity and contentment. Many spiritual traditions emphasize forgiveness as a path to spiritual growth and enlightenment. Forgiveness enables you to transcend ego-driven desires and align with higher principles of love, compassion, and forgiveness.

Carrying grudges keeps you tethered to the past, preventing you from fully embracing the present moment and moving forward with your life. Forgiveness liberates you from the burdens of the past, allowing you to live more fully in the present. Forgiveness is an act of strength, not weakness. It empowers you to take control of your own emotions and reactions, rather than being controlled by past hurts and resentments.

In essence, forgiveness *nourishes* the soul by promoting healing, compassion, inner peace, and personal growth. It is a powerful tool for living a more fulfilling and enriching life. In many religious traditions, including Christianity, forgiveness is intricately tied to the concept of divine forgiveness. According to Christian belief, forgiving others is not only a moral imperative but also a reflection of one's relationship with God.

Several passages in the Bible, such as Matthew 6:14-15 and Matthew 18:21-22, emphasize the connection between forgiving others and receiving forgiveness from God. These teachings underscore the importance of forgiveness in the Christian faith. Jesus Christ serves as the ultimate model of forgiveness in Christianity. His teachings and actions consistently emphasize forgiveness, even in the face of betrayal and persecution. The crucifixion itself is often interpreted as an act of divine forgiveness, offering redemption to humanity.

Jesus frequently used parables and teachings to illustrate the importance of forgiveness. For example, the Parable of the Prodigal Son (Luke 15:11-32) highlights the compassion and forgiveness of God toward repentant sinners, encouraging followers to emulate this forgiveness in their own lives.

Some interpretations of Christian theology suggest that divine forgiveness is conditional upon human forgiveness. In other words, those who forgive others demonstrate their understanding of God's forgiveness and are more receptive to receiving it themselves. Alongside forgiveness, repentance and confession are central aspects of seeking divine forgiveness in Christianity. The acknowledgment of wrongdoing, sincere remorse, and commitment to change are considered essential steps toward reconciliation with God.

Ultimately, forgiveness in Christianity is rooted in God's grace and mercy. While forgiveness may be conditional upon human actions, it is ultimately a gift bestowed by God out of love and compassion for humanity. Interpretations of forgiveness and divine forgiveness may vary among different Christian denominations and individual believers. However, the overarching principle remains that forgiveness of others is closely linked to the forgiveness one receives from God in Christian theology.

Clara's Journey

Once upon a time, in a small town nestled between rolling hills and whispering forests, there lived a woman named Clara. Clara carried within her a heavy burden of resentment toward her mother, Maria. From as far back as she could remember, Clara felt that her mother's actions had caused her nothing but misery.

Maria was a stern woman, raised in the strict traditions of her own upbringing. She had always expected perfection from Clara, pushing her to excel in every aspect of her life. Whether it was academics, sports, or social interactions, Maria's expectations weighed heavily on Clara's shoulders, leaving her feeling inadequate and unworthy.

As Clara grew older, her resentment deepened. She blamed her mother for every failure, every missed opportunity, every moment of unhappiness. She felt trapped by the shadows of her past, unable to break free from the cycle of blame and bitterness.

Years passed, and Clara's heart grew heavier with each passing day. She longed for liberation from the shackles of her own judgment, but she could not find it within herself to forgive her mother. It seemed an impossible task, an insurmountable mountain blocking her path to peace.

But then, one day, something changed. Clara received news that her mother was gravely ill and had been hospitalized. In that moment,

Clara's walls of resentment began to crumble. She realized that life was too short to hold onto grudges, too precious to waste on bitterness and regret.

With a heavy heart, Clara visited her mother in the hospital. As she stood by Maria's bedside, watching her frail form, she saw not the stern figure of her childhood, but a vulnerable woman in need of love and compassion. In that moment, Clara's heart softened, and she found the strength to forgive.

In the days that followed, Clara and Maria began to rebuild their relationship. They spoke openly and honestly, sharing their fears, their regrets, and their hopes for the future. With each conversation, the walls between them crumbled further, until they were no longer mother and daughter, but two souls bound together by love and understanding.

And as Clara embraced her mother, tears streaming down her cheeks, she felt a weight lift from her shoulders. In that moment of forgiveness, she found the liberation she had been searching for all her life. No longer bound by judgment or resentment, Clara was free to embrace the beauty of life, to cherish the moments of joy and togetherness that she had once taken for granted.

From that day forward, Clara lived each moment with gratitude in her heart, knowing that the greatest gift of all was the ability to forgive, to let go of the past, and to embrace the boundless possibilities of the future. And in her newfound freedom, she found a peace that would guide her on her journey through life, forevermore.

13

Forgiveness Affects Your Mind

13 Chapter Forgiveness Affects Your Mind

Forgiveness can have a profound impact on your mental well-being. When you forgive someone, you release yourself from the negative emotions associated with the hurt or offense they caused you. This release can lead to reduced feelings of anger, resentment, and bitterness, which can weigh heavily on your mental health. Instead, forgiveness often brings about feelings of peace, empathy, and understanding.

Mentally, forgiveness can also lead to greater resilience and a sense of empowerment. By choosing to forgive, you take control of your emotions and responses, rather than allowing past grievances to continue to dictate how you feel and behave. This can result in increased self-esteem and a more positive outlook on life.

Moreover, forgiveness can improve your relationships with others. When you forgive someone, it often fosters reconciliation and promotes healthier interactions. This can lead to greater social support and a stronger sense of connection with others, which are important factors for mental well-being.

Overall, forgiveness can have a transformative effect on your mental health, helping you to let go of negativity, cultivate inner peace, and nurture healthier relationships with others. Also, Forgiveness can contribute to clearer thinking. When you hold onto feelings of resentment, anger, or bitterness toward someone who has wronged you, it can cloud your judgment and impair your ability to think rationally.

These negative emotions can create mental clutter, distracting you from focusing on other aspects of your life and making it difficult to see situations objectively.

However, when you choose to forgive, you free yourself from the burden of those negative emotions. This can create space in your mind for clearer, more rational thinking. Without the weight of grudges or grievances holding you back, you may find it easier to concentrate, make decisions, and problem-solve effectively.

Forgiveness can help you let go of rumination and mental loops associated with past hurts, allowing you to focus more on the present and future. Moreover, forgiveness often involves gaining perspective and understanding, which can enhance your ability to see situations from different angles and consider alternative viewpoints. This expanded perspective can lead to more nuanced and insightful thinking, enabling you to approach challenges with greater clarity and wisdom.

Forgiveness can play a significant role in fostering clearer thinking by freeing your mind from the distortions caused by negative emotions and promoting a more balanced and open-minded perspective. Basically, forgiveness is a transformative process that promotes healing at the deepest levels of the soul, relationships, and emotions. It allows individuals to experience inner peace, restore damaged relationships, and cultivate emotional well-being and resilience.

Michael's Journey

In the heart of a bustling city, hidden away from the chaos of the streets, stood a towering institution with walls that seemed to stretch endlessly into the sky. Within those walls, amidst the echoing halls and whispered secrets, resided a man named Michael.

Michael had spent the better part of his life within the confines of the institution, trapped in a prison of his own making. He carried with him a burden heavier than any chains, a burden of shame and guilt that weighed him down with each passing day.

As a child, Michael had been placed in an orphanage, a place that was meant to be a sanctuary but had become a nightmare. There, he had endured unspeakable horrors at the hands of those who were supposed to care for him, leaving scars that ran deeper than any physical wound.

For years, Michael had carried the weight of his past, haunted by memories that refused to fade. He blamed himself for the abuse he had suffered, believing that he was somehow responsible for the pain inflicted upon him. The shame and guilt gnawed at his soul, consuming him from the inside out.

But then, one day, something shifted within Michael. It was as if a spark had been ignited within the darkness of his despair, a glimmer of hope amidst the shadows. He realized that he could not continue to carry the burden of his past, that he could not keep allowing the ghosts of his childhood to haunt him forever.

With a newfound determination, Michael made a decision that would change his life forever. He chose to forgive. He chose to forgive those who had hurt him, to release the anger and bitterness that had held him captive for so long. It was not an easy decision, nor was it one made lightly, but it was a decision born out of a deep desire for freedom.

And as Michael let go of his anger and resentment, something remarkable happened. The walls that had surrounded him for so long began to crumble, the chains that had bound him loosening their grip. He felt a weight lift from his shoulders, a weight that he had carried for far too long.

With each passing day, Michael felt himself growing stronger, his spirit renewed by the power of forgiveness. The shame and guilt that had once consumed him began to fade, replaced by a sense of peace and liberation that he had never known before.

And as Michael walked out of the institution, his steps light and free, he knew that he was finally free from the demons of his past. He had found forgiveness, and in doing so, he had found freedom.

14

Forgiveness Affects Your Health

14 Chapter Forgiveness Affects Your Health

Holding onto grudges and harboring resentment can contribute to chronic stress, which is linked to a variety of health problems, including hypertension, heart disease, and weakened immune function. Forgiveness reduces stress by releasing negative emotions and promoting emotional well-being.

Studies have shown that practicing forgiveness can lead to lower blood pressure levels. Chronic anger and hostility are associated with higher blood pressure, while forgiveness helps to mitigate these negative effects by promoting relaxation and reducing physiological arousal.

Chronic stress and negative emotions can weaken the immune system, making individuals more susceptible to illness and infection. Forgiveness strengthens the immune system by reducing stress levels and promoting positive emotions, which in turn enhances immune function.

Forgiveness is associated with improved mental health outcomes, including reduced symptoms of depression, anxiety, and psychological distress. Letting go of grudges and negative emotions can alleviate psychological suffering and promote emotional well-being.

Healthy relationships are essential for overall well-being, and forgiveness plays a crucial role in maintaining and strengthening relationships. By fostering empathy, compassion, and reconciliation, forgiveness contributes to healthier and more supportive social connections, which are beneficial for mental and physical health.

Chronic anger and hostility are risk factors for cardiovascular disease, including heart attacks and strokes. Forgiveness has been linked to improved cardiovascular health by reducing anger and hostility levels, lowering blood pressure, and promoting overall heart health.

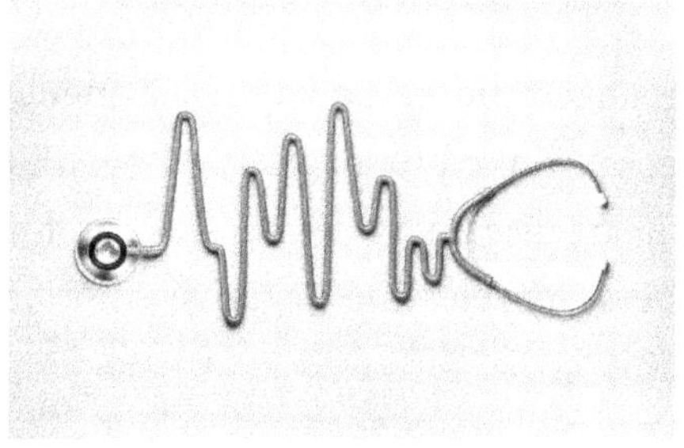

Some research suggests that forgiveness may be associated with a longer life expectancy. By reducing stress, promoting emotional well-being, and improving physical health outcomes, forgiveness may contribute to a longer and healthier life.

Overall, forgiveness is not only beneficial for interpersonal relationships and emotional well-being but also has tangible effects on physical health outcomes. By releasing negative emotions, reducing stress, and promoting positive social connections, forgiveness contributes to a healthier and more fulfilling life.

Evelyn's Journey

In a quaint suburban neighborhood, tucked away behind a picket fence and blooming garden, lived an elderly woman named Evelyn. With her silver hair and gentle smile, she was the picture of grace and warmth. But behind closed doors, Evelyn bore a burden that weighed heavy on her heart.

Every time her middle-aged son, Daniel, entered the house, Evelyn's blood pressure would spike, sending her heart racing and her head pounding. For years, she had suffered in silence, unable to understand why the mere presence of her own flesh and blood filled her with such dread.

Her daughter, Sarah, grew increasingly concerned as she witnessed her mother's health deteriorate with each passing day. Determined to uncover the cause of Evelyn's distress, Sarah began to pay closer attention to her interactions with Daniel.

It didn't take long for Sarah to discover the truth lurking beneath the surface. Through careful observation and subtle questioning, she learned that Daniel had been physically abusing their mother, inflicting pain, and suffering behind closed doors.

Sarah was devastated by the revelation, her heart breaking for the mother she loved and the brother she once trusted. But she knew that she had to act quickly to protect Evelyn from further harm.

With courage and determination, Sarah confronted Daniel, demanding answers, and holding him accountable for his actions. At first, Daniel denied everything, his words laced with excuses and defensiveness. But as Sarah pressed him further, he could no longer hide from the truth.

In the days that followed, Evelyn faced a difficult decision. She struggled to come to terms with the betrayal she had endured at the hands of her own son, torn between anger and heartache. But deep within her soul, she found the strength to do something unexpected.

Evelyn chose to forgive.

It was not an easy decision, nor was it one made lightly. But Evelyn knew that holding onto anger and resentment would only poison her spirit and darken her soul. She knew that forgiveness was the key to unlocking the chains that bound her heart.

As Evelyn embraced forgiveness, something miraculous began to happen. The walls around her heart began to crumble, replaced by a sense of peace and healing that she had thought was lost forever. The weight of her pain lifted from her shoulders, replaced by a newfound sense of freedom and liberation.

With each passing day, Evelyn grew stronger, her spirit renewed by the power of forgiveness. She no longer lived in fear of her son's presence, for she had found the courage to let go of the past and embrace the beauty of the present.

And as Evelyn looked to the future, she knew that she would face whatever challenges came her way with grace and resilience. For she had learned that forgiveness was not a sign of weakness, but a testament to the strength of the human spirit. And in forgiving her son, Evelyn had found the healing and redemption she had so desperately longed for.

15

How Unforgiveness Affects You

15 Chapter How Unforgiveness Affects You

Unforgiveness, on the other hand, can have several negative effects on individuals' well-being, relationships, and overall quality of life. Holding onto grudges and resentment can contribute to chronic stress, which has detrimental effects on both mental and physical health. Persistent stress can lead to anxiety, depression, insomnia, and other stress-related disorders.

Unforgiveness often perpetuates negative emotions such as anger, bitterness, and resentment. These emotions can consume individuals' thoughts and feelings, leading to heightened levels of unhappiness, irritability, and emotional distress.

Unforgiveness can damage relationships by fostering hostility, mistrust, and communication breakdowns. It creates barriers to reconciliation and prevents individuals from experiencing the intimacy and connection that come with forgiveness.

Chronic unforgiveness is associated with various health problems, including hypertension, cardiovascular disease, weakened immune function, and even chronic pain conditions. The physiological stress response triggered by unforgiveness can have long-term implications for overall health and well-being.

Unforgiveness is closely linked to poor mental health outcomes, including symptoms of depression, anxiety, and psychological distress. It can undermine individuals' sense of self-worth, increase feelings of helplessness, and contribute to a negative outlook on life.

Unforgiveness diminishes individuals' overall quality of life by limiting their ability to experience joy, peace, and fulfillment. It keeps them tethered to past hurts and prevents them from fully engaging in the present moment and future opportunities.

For individuals with spiritual or religious beliefs, unforgiveness can create spiritual distress and conflict. It may lead to feelings of guilt, shame, and spiritual disconnection, as forgiveness is often regarded as a fundamental principle of many spiritual traditions.

Unforgiveness perpetuates a cycle of negativity and resentment, both internally and in relationships. It can lead to a pattern of holding onto grudges, seeking revenge, and perpetuating conflict, which ultimately hinders personal growth and relational harmony.

Overall, unforgiveness is detrimental to individuals' physical health, mental well-being, relationships, and spiritual growth. It perpetuates a cycle of negativity and suffering, hindering individuals' ability to experience peace, healing, and fulfillment in their lives.

Emily's Journey

In the heart of a bustling city, amidst the noise and chaos of everyday life, there lived a young woman named Emily. With her bright eyes and infectious smile, she seemed to radiate warmth and joy to all who crossed her path. But beneath her cheerful facade lay a heart burdened by unforgiveness.

Emily had been wronged in the past, hurt by someone she had trusted with all her heart. The pain of betrayal cut deep, leaving scars that seemed to fester with each passing day. Unable to let go of her anger and resentment, Emily retreated into a world of bitterness and isolation, closing herself off from the possibility of healing and redemption.

As the years went by, Emily's unforgiveness began to take its toll not only on herself but on those around her. Her relationships grew strained, her once vibrant personality overshadowed by a cloud of negativity. Friends and loved ones watched helplessly as Emily spiraled deeper into misery, unable to reach her through the walls she had built around her heart.

Even strangers felt the weight of Emily's unforgiving spirit, as her sharp words and cold demeanor cast a shadow over every interaction. The joy and kindness she had once embodied seemed to fade away, replaced by a sense of emptiness and despair.

With a heavy heart, Emily made a decision that would change her life forever. She chose to forgive. It was not an easy decision, nor was it one made lightly, but it was a decision born out of a deep desire for freedom and healing

16

Conclusion

16 Chapter Conclusion

Forgiveness is not limited to personal growth and healing. It has the potential to ignite social change, foster unity, and transform our communities. By embracing forgiveness in our relationships, trauma healing, addiction recovery, parenting, workplace dynamics, criminal justice practices, and cultural contexts, we unlock the transformative power of forgiveness and pave the way for a more compassionate and united world.

Throughout this book, we have discussed the transformative power of forgiveness in various aspects of our lives. From relationships to religious and spiritual contexts, from healing trauma to personal growth, from addiction recovery to parenting and family dynamics, forgiveness has been proven to bring about spiritual freedom and inner peace. It is a concept that resonates with people of all ages and backgrounds, including parents, children, grandparents, wives, husbands, and individuals from diverse walks of life.

Forgiveness is not an easy path to embark upon. It requires immense strength, courage, and vulnerability. It can be a long and challenging journey, but the rewards it brings are immeasurable. By embracing forgiveness, we can release the burden of resentment, anger, and pain that weighs us down. We free ourselves from the chains of the past and open ourselves up to a future filled with love, compassion, and joy.

In relationships, forgiveness is the key to repairing and rebuilding bonds that have been damaged. It allows us to let go of grudges and find ways to empathize with and understand one another. Through forgiveness, we can create spaces for healing, growth, and deeper connections with our loved ones.

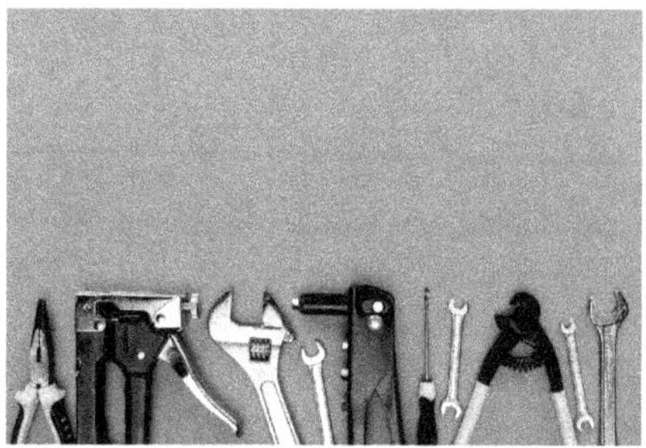

In religious and spiritual contexts, forgiveness is a core principle that promotes harmony, compassion, and unity. It leads us on a journey towards enlightenment, helping us cultivate a deeper connection with our higher selves and the divine. Through forgiveness, we can transcend our ego and tap into a greater sense of peace and wholeness.

Forgiveness is also a powerful tool in healing trauma. By forgiving those who have hurt us, we release ourselves from the grip of the past and allow ourselves to heal. It is a process that requires immense self-compassion and self-care, but through forgiveness, we can find the strength to move forward and reclaim our lives.

Furthermore, forgiveness plays a vital role in self-growth and personal development. It allows us to let go of self-limiting beliefs and embrace our true potential. By forgiving ourselves for past mistakes, we create space for personal transformation and growth.

In addiction recovery, forgiveness is an essential step towards healing and breaking free from the cycle of addiction. It helps us release shame, guilt, and self-blame, allowing us to rebuild our lives and embrace a future of sobriety and well-being.

Forgiveness also has a profound impact on parenting and family dynamics. By teaching our children the importance of forgiveness, we foster a culture of empathy, understanding, and love within our families. It helps us break generational patterns of pain and create nurturing environments where our children can thrive.

In the workplace, forgiveness promotes healthier relationships and a more positive work environment. It allows us to let go of workplace conflicts and focus on collaboration, productivity, and personal growth.

In criminal justice and restorative justice practices, forgiveness offers a path towards healing, reconciliation, and rehabilitation. It helps individuals find closure and move forward with their lives, while also fostering a sense of empathy and understanding within communities.

Forgiveness has the power to transcend cultural and societal contexts. It breaks down barriers, promotes understanding, and fosters unity among diverse communities. It is a universal concept that speaks to the core of our humanity.

Moreover, we have also acknowledged the importance of forgiveness in religious and spiritual contexts. Many individuals seek solace and guidance in their faith and understanding forgiveness within these contexts can be transformative and enlightening.

Another significant aspect we have covered in this book is the role of forgiveness in healing trauma. Traumatic experiences can leave deep emotional wounds, and forgiveness can be a powerful tool in the recovery process. We explore different approaches and techniques that can aid individuals in their journey towards healing and self-growth.

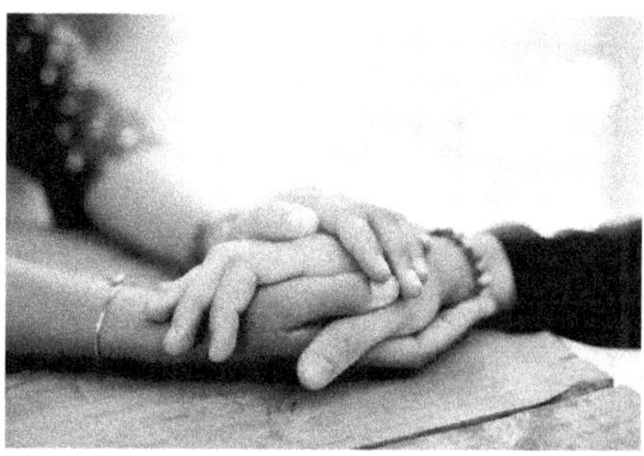

Furthermore, we delve into the connection between forgiveness and addiction recovery. Addiction can strain relationships and create immense pain for both the individual and their loved ones. By exploring forgiveness in this context, we aim to assist individuals in their path to recovery and reconciliation.

Additionally, we discussed forgiveness in parenting and family dynamics. Forgiveness plays a crucial role in maintaining healthy relationships within families, and we provide practical insights and strategies for parents and children alike.

In conclusion, embracing forgiveness is a transformative journey that leads to spiritual freedom and inner peace. It is a path that can be walked by parents, children, grandparents, wives, husbands, and individuals from all walks of life. By choosing forgiveness, we choose love, compassion, and healing. We release ourselves from the chains of the past and open ourselves up to a future filled with joy, harmony, and ful1llment.

May forgiveness guide you on your journey towards spiritual freedom and inner peace.

17

ABOUT THE AUTHOR

17 ABOUT THE AUTHOR

My own odyssey with forgiveness began with personal experiences that tested the boundaries of my heart and soul. Through moments of anguish, resentment, and ultimately, liberation, I embarked on a quest to understand the intricate dynamics of forgiveness — its complexities, its challenges, and its boundless capacity to heal.

In this book, I delve deep into the multifaceted nature of forgiveness, offering insights, reflections, and practical guidance for readers embarking on their own forgiveness journey. Drawing from biblical research and spiritual wisdom, I illuminate the transformative power of forgiveness and its profound impact on relationships, personal well-being, and collective healing.

Through thought-provoking exercises, meditations, and reflective prompts, I invite readers to embark on a soul-stirring exploration of forgiveness — not as a one-time act, but as an ongoing practice of compassion, empathy, and self-discovery. Whether you seek solace from past wounds, yearn for reconciliation with others, or aspire to cultivate a deeper sense of inner peace, this book offers a guiding light on the path to forgiveness.

Beyond the pages of this book lies a greater mission — a mission to foster a culture of empathy, reconciliation, and healing in a world often besieged by conflict and division. Through speaking engagements, workshops, and community outreach initiatives, I strive to ignite conversations about forgiveness, promote understanding across differences, and inspire collective action towards a more compassionate and harmonious society.

Join the Journey:

I invite you to join me on this transformative journey towards forgiveness — a journey that transcends boundaries, bridges divides, and restores the very essence of our humanity. Together, let us embrace the power of forgiveness to heal, to transform, and to create a more compassionate world for generations to come.

With gratitude and hope,
Susette O'Neal

Author of "Forgiveness: Set your Spirit Free"